The Built Environment

The Built Environment

Emily Hasler

For Hannah

with huge thanks
& admiration.

[signature]

Keats House
May 2018

First published 2018 by
Liverpool University Press
4 Cambridge Street
Liverpool
L69 7ZU

Copyright © 2018 Liverpool University Press

The right of Emily Hasler to be identified as the author of this book
has been asserted by her in accordance with the Copyright, Designs
and Patents Act 1988.

British Library Cataloguing-in-Publication data
A British Library CIP record is available

ISBN 978-1-78694-104-6 softback

Typeset by Carnegie Book Production, Lancaster
Printed and bound in Poland by Booksfactory.co.uk

For my parents

There must be many exciting properties of matter that we cannot know because we have no way to know them. Yet, with what we have, what wealth! I add to it each time I go to the mountain— the eye sees what it didn't see before, or sees in a new way what it had already seen. So the ear, the other senses. It is an experience that grows; undistinguished days add their part, and now and then, unpredictable and unforgettable, come the hours when heaven and earth fall away and one sees a new creation.

Nan Shepherd, *The Living Mountain*

Rivers and fields no more just happen than do buildings...

Jonathan Meades, *Father to the Man*

Contents

On Headed Paper

What I've been meaning to mention is the folding machine;
how it's truly a marvellous thing and I want you to see it.
And I want us to take it to the beach or to visit Stonehenge.

The noise it makes when I set it to work is loud. Like the over-zealous
in the pub it wants to be heard. How I love that sex grunt,
that cha-cha of doing. Tap out the pain. I am repeating myself

but look, the folding machine again. It's not trying or trying not to
distract itself. Trapped in every second of me is the folding machine.
I want to put it beyond use. One day I'll throw it into the grave

of my loved ones. It is so good at what it does. I tried to re-invent
the folding machine. There must be a first bit, a second, connections,
cogs. It's in me, stuck between my head and heart and my other

unnumbered, unlabelled parts. Reassemble and repeat. Sing: we love
the folding machine. It must be something like the sun, or the moon
at least. The noise. The casing of it! A miracle. The papers spilling

perfectly at the end. An end to repetition and patience (which is pain).
Someone made the folding machine. I tried to re-invent, repeat.
That clever, co-operative order of parts, that do and do and make

no apology for being one way and then another, that try and fail.
But try not to fail. Sing too loudly. Be exact then not so, fixed then broken,
need instruction. I'm waiting for it. I'm waiting for this thing to exist.

The Built Environment

a waste and ownerless place

Botolph

There is in this place as little as can be
imagined, so things stand in for each other:
metal turns to wood, wood
to bone, ruins to wrack—
in this already regretting wind,
both scourge and the salt to heal it.

The air is most of the materials
needed for the church and the best
of the gutting fire. This creamy crag
is a flushwork of creatures, late of the land.
Moving mudstone is a tracery of bubbles
forming, bursting, flat and still as water,
thick and permanent as the first render—
a thin layer that dries as it cracks.

Sub-architecture

You can't blame us for our home towns with their proliferating
   semis,
the pebble-dash and exposed red-brick uniformly imperfect.

Since my translocation I see it, on Google Earth, the squamous
   look
the roofs have. The scabbed pavement where they put in

and then took out the beech, because they planted *the wrong sort*
of trees. They and their roots had to go. Insertions. Deletions.

My avenue. Come to the point. What hedges planted, trimmed,
removed? How would you describe the shape of the end, dead end,

and its turning-slash-parking room? The way it floods when it rains
all afternoon? It's like… we're incompatible. Because? Houses can't

shut their windows, can't open their doors and aren't at all like us.
Except, they too must worry about what's going on inside. The
   shuffling

of objects, the changing of rooms. And I'm sorry houses, what a
   price to pay;
to lose your character! All for the love of warmth and/or economy.

So cells in sunlight, shot aerially, glint—not fully changed, but,
probabilistically, resigned to change. I'm sorry town, I see you now,

browed and beating. Unregulated and still spreading. They got you
on a good day, waiting—as if that was living. But it is living.

It's not our fault, we're simple and malefic. I think we can do
   better. Well.

Bernini's Apollo and Daphne

A statue in the Villa Borghese, Rome

I fooled the sculptor—thinking he could
catch my undying trick. How did I
become a container and pour myself into it

at the same time? I flowed from marble,
I flowed back into it. I'll endure, perpetually
tightening the tiny gimbals in each

foliated fingertip. Staying still is unceasing,
always becoming: girl, god, stone, tree, sculptor.
And these who come to stand, circle, stand—

do they know they have forgotten themselves
a moment too long? Moments are large as villas,
parks, mythologies, centuries of Art. Thoughts

run through me like a fountain, water in constant
escape—which is no escape.

What Gretel Knows

Gretel knows what to say to the boy who thinks we're saved.
Gretel knows, put a girl in water and she'll drown; boil it,
she'll cook. Gretel knows there's no salvation; only storage,
refrigeration, freezing. A fairytale of Tupperware, stained
and scratched, sudded beside the sink. Even old crones
have to eat. We be fat. We be lean. Gretel knows it's just
a change of state, conduction of heat. Gretel knows
how we swell and settle like dough with weight of air, time.
The child hacked from the wolf's stomach, pulled from the womb,
taken from the oven or the pot. But Gretel knows it is too late.
The ingredients in us activate. A raising. Our edges puff and blur,
give and take of the world about us. It doesn't matter, Gretel told him,
she knows that the house is cake for fuck's sake. The earth
is seasoning. Our sweet flesh is so tender it flakes between
our fingers. Gretel knows. That the wicked stepmother,
the old crone, Baba Yaga, me—Gretel—we are all the same.
Archetypal and obsessed with our stomachs. Gretel says:
This is the bread that broke the body. This is my body: take it. Eat.
This is the tongue that licked the bowl of the cement mixer clean.

Katana

It's an exact art; to cheat two types of steel
to turn them to face one another then heat,
hammer and heat. To fold and fold again:

eight times, sixteen times over. There,
it starts to feel—in its united heart—
that it is strong, light, supple, hard.

So flexible this silver tongue, this collusion
of men and metals. Now it acts as though
it were always one. Cooled too quick

to rethink its false society of parts. I could tell
how the air rings when the sword slices through.
The sound: true. The balance true, and the shine

too—which was two weeks' work.

Where the Swimming Pool Was

is a thick and cared-for set of hedges
that hold no water in

but suggest the wet with gleaming leaves
and perhaps their height

is the former depth into which we
pretend to dive

as we had seen the unabashed dead do
in looped home movie

smiling and seeming to learn each movement over
they offered them to the camera

and in my mind I rehearse actions
assess that were I to

decant myself evenly and all at once
the hedge could take

my lain but not my standing weight
the way I lay

now in simulated float on the grass that is
where the water was

hammocky between two thoughts
there is

a swimming pool there is no swimming pool
a barely noticed

clutch and release a balancing of the blue sky
with eyes closed

and the possibility of clouds in my mind
I cannot drift

only imagine knocking between the fore
and back legs of a chair

until I am told not to

A False Winter

We kept waiting. The wind was up.
Rain rallied. The plumbing griped.
And we were just large, disappointed
stomachs devouring ourselves
and one boxset after another.

Murder mysteries were best: eccentrics
in scenes with solid aesthetics—and often snow.
Evil seems to incubate in its warm hollows,
crimes obscured then shown up red.
We felt guilty for wanting deaths,

then for wanting snow. And guilty
for not knowing why, or what it would mean—
but thinking that if it begins and lays,
if it could consolidate, make it through
a night, a next day...

We lost all cravings but remained hungry,
enormously weary but never ready for bed.
We lay sleepless until we woke to dark
and the sense of the unsolved case. We looked
to our windows as if they were TVs.

Tammasmass E'en

It's a sore soul that cannot lay down tools
or use the Yule to its proper end; strong drink,
food. Five nights afore and the fires light no fretting
of hands at wool, no kneading of dough. No,
I but pretend at northern-islandness, an imagined
Viking kink in my cells. I inhabit this for a while,
alone. All being well. All not being well. It's time.
The earth feigns death and we too must learn
not-doing. The very baby unborn cries 'oh dul! dul!'
and doesn't stop to wonder where it found its words.

Notes: A Monumental Brass

1. Brand, T.C., 'An Uneven History: Monumental Brasses and Stone Ledgers in English Church Floors' (Oxford 1982).

2. Husbands are almost always specified on women's grave inscriptions.

3. Having no husbands, and therefore no sons, we remained daughters, sisters.

4. It is less than one-quarter the size of the memorial placed to Elizabeth Etchingham's father and grandparents, one of several factors suggesting economies were taken in the production of this memorial. On the reverse is an inscription to Thomas Austin, son of a London mercer, who died in 1405. Although we cannot be certain that the brass's placement in the south chancel is original, the location would be of a piece with these cost-saving measures.

5. The depictions of the women bear the conventional signs of unmarried status. Elizabeth Etchingham is smaller and her flowing hair shows her as a nubile maiden, whereas the larger size, coifed hair and uncovered head of Agnes Oxenbridge tell us that she was older but still maidenly.

6. K. M. Phillips, 'Maidenhood as the Perfect Age of Woman's Life', in *Young Medieval Women*, K. J. Lewis, N. J. Menuge and K. M. Phillips (New York 1999), 1–24.

7. 94 per cent of aristocratic women made their careers as wives, mothers and widows. However, singleness was not unknown.

8. Gatskill, James, 'As she were mine sister': *Extra-familial Female Relationships in Late Medieval England* (London 1991).

9. As Paul Binski has noted, 'The turning of figures on their axis enabled the intimacy of the marriage to be expressed'. Although the move to showing the female figure in semi-profile is sometimes attributed to a desire to better illustrate elaborate headdresses.

10. I have not found a single example of a design in which the husband is turned towards a front-facing wife.

11. Neither the artisan nor anyone else seemed to have considered this affective turn unsuited for a female couple or unseemly for their families.

12. I have learnt to hear, to feel almost, the particular fall of your foot on the stair, the cracking of the air as your gown brushes mine.

13. Women's gowns on late-15th-century brasses generally fall in folds so deep, stable and balanced that they seem to root the women to the ground rather than propel them in one direction or another. Yet, the gowns of Elizabeth Etchingham and Agnes Oxenbridge were arranged in such a way as illustrate their movement towards each other.

14. The way our little fingers divine each other beneath the table cloth.

15. The nature of their relationship is anyone's guess, although the possibilities are not infinite.

16. As with all conventions, there were exceptions.

17. Medieval engravers were known as 'marblers', because engraving initially began with brass letters embedded in marble pavements and because brasses were set into marble slabs. I use the less confusing 'engravers' here.

Inscription

Judith Eyre, 'who died much lamented,
in the 35th Year of her Age,
in consequence of having accidentally
swallow'd a Pin.' What can we know
of her life? Within: her organs greasy grey
as filmed ponds, her blood taking the routes
Harvey mapped. No thread to follow,
only the needle—so perfectly made to make
an opening, to find a way. And this is the
only way—we dart in, so unlikely
and then so definite. Led by our finest part,
it is but narrowly we escape into our futures
(though obvious the marks upon the past).

Cambridge Primitive

after Alfred Wallis

In the seaside of a white room with good, large windows
we talked about that light,
and all the angles we like and dislike.

We were a pretty crude picture of happiness—
as simple as a shell, as a harbour
with houses in green and pink,

with a whole economy based on fish.
Green and pink and silver fish. Heaps of them.
I have a whole fleet of thoughts about this but

Look at the houses! Look at the ship!
Not at all the right way up...
And we are not so near the sea

though the light makes us think otherwise.
There's nothing between here and the Urals,
nothing but the large, flat sea—oh and heaps of fish of course.

On Reading the Meaning of 'Falchion'
in an Encyclopaedia

A 'falchion', from the Old French
is a sword. It cuts swathes like the Persian scimitar
and digs through bowels as the Chinese Dao does.
But it is its own, itself: a sword, from the Old French.
A specific means of death.

The incision that was made becomes apparent
and blood hurries to the surface after the mid-air cartoon pause.
The stench of blood undrying. Battles rewind, soldiers come to
     life.
And what you were saying was that people were dying
on the end of this particular kind of knife?

Knowledge is the great unstaunchable wound.
A sword is a sword is a sword. But
what sort? And a word, yes, means nothing by itself,
is simply a point which impales, pins a specimen of reality to the
     paper
so we might squint and imagine how it once flew.

And now they're everywhere, and when someone wields the word
I hold my hands up. I say, yes, a sword, from the Old French. Yet
     before
I must have run through many pages, escaping harm, not knowing
the pointed syllables had sharp edges and that I scanned so close
     to danger
and failed to notice the sun catching at the quilloned crossguard.

Wish You Were Here

picking this postcard
I recall what you told me
about Mondrian
that he hated green
so deeply
he cut off friends
who disagreed
remembering this is
almost to be with you
passing through
doorless openings
to locate
a familiar piece
the truth is
it is simple
but it must be arranged
on trains
I always think
of you and how I read
that Piet although
he hated green
was moved by
rural scenery
when seen from
a moving train
but only because
of the way
the telegraph poles
intersect the landscape
yet this is only
a recollection
of what his friend

thought and that
itself in writing
to another friend
see how we must
cut away at the world
till we get to the fact
get back go back
directions are
a sort of simplification
if you follow me
to a room with
a vacant bench
and a masterpiece
it is basic primary
it's simple
we must find
ways to meet

Othona

The middle of nowhere is an exact place.
The horizons are endless and my feet ache
just thinking about it. Let's sit here a while,
it's warm and pleasant between glaciations.

A good spot. We'll see them marching across
the sea—what water bears it may also
carry away. I can wait. See, we're not the first
to decide to build from nothing.

Potpourri

I don't know who put the cups on mats or the converted
garden dead in bowls where they stay, incorruptible
and mute as saints. I am not sure where, but the air
was a mist, full with talc, pricked with hairspray's
lingering tack. *Please, sit.* Write down all that can
be remembered on this scented page. And *by the time
we're done you won't recognise the place.* Won't stay put:
sweeps up, plumps cushions, shuffles mess away. Worrying more
and more in to the heaving drawer of the sideboard.

Check the corners of your lint-lined brain. Can you at least say,
what is the word in the way of the word *on the tip of my tongue?*
By the window you can see it: the false depths in polished wood,
the creases in your morning face, how thrown together a day is.

The Animal in Motion

on Eadweard Muybridge

Those poor hostages, trapped in their sequential cells;
forced to walk or run, to climb, to sit then stand,
stand then sit. How miserable the captive animal is,
worried away—till they lose hair, presence, weight—
with the fret of knowing they are being watched.
Their every moving part dissected. It seems a wonder
anyone *does* anything. Reduced to one action the body
strains to bend and lift, to step from the frame.

Beyond the frame: the black that is non-happening.
Deep as a canyon, what it is between. A space
with the capacity of sleep, the near darkness of a blink.
Barely noticed and then dismissed. The moment
is neither metrical nor imperial, neither ends nor begins.
Each step's a crime: the before and after and frontier within.

Cartography for Beginners

First of all, you will need to choose the correct blue
to indicate water. This should not be *too watery*.
You must remember: people do not like wet feet.
If there is no water to indicate, no matter,
you must still elect a blue. Let me recommend
eggshell, at a push, azure. Choose a symbol
for church/temple/mosque/synagogue. Choose
a symbol for pub. Dedicate your life
to the twin and warring gods of Precision
and Wild Abandon. People do not like
to be lost. Buy Mandelbrot's 1967 paper
on the coastline paradox, put it on the highest shelf,
but get a stepladder. Take a little licence with rivers,
especially their curves and estuaries. Add
an oxbow lake if at all possible. If the area you
are mapping has no sea/lakes/rivers/streams,
I have to question why you are bothering. You
won't get to use that lovely blue you spent so long
deciding upon. Do the Norfolk fens instead. Better
yet, East Anglia in its future state, quite utterly
submerged like a sodden Constable. Come on,
get your coat, I'll show you. You won't need your shoes.

'Grasmere Lake'

A tautology, yes, but then the pedant's tut
ignores precisely the fact: some things deserve
the slip of double affirmation, being twice named
for good reason—once for the mere width, once
more for those hidden depths. Gasp not
at the reiteration but the escapology,
the trick by which we entangle further to detach,
the reason for the taut surface and infinite trapdoors
which open only once and promptly close fast.

The Valley of the Stour
with Dedham in the Distance

o England, the time we thought
your cows were cricketers
the sun was blinking round
like an uncle saying o o o
very quietly to his feet
the fizzed out grass
beery river thick with weeds
water meadows endless even
the church kept winking
on the horizon popping between
poplars bending willows
standard oaks a tower
too grand a digression ups
downs trade booms mills
puritans buried by law in wool
soil smoothed to subtle tumuli
soft buttered decline a boat
buffing a bank in evening light
the tower again Constable added it in
if he could quite right you must
fix a scene with something
pretend churches stay put
place your men Captain
arrange the gaps the cows stood
circled intent groupings
of white curdling in the corner
of the eye cricket end of season
tea the milk still settling

The Henry Hudson Bridge

1.

The estuary's deepened by centuries of concern.

Massive and slow, lowing like cattle, the ships draw our eyes
down the channel. What a silly shallop a word is—

but the names they give these enormous container ships!
The Henry Hudson Bridge: a boat named for a bridge,
named for a man. We looked him up. A time of trade over nation,
passages. Belief in progress. Simple forward movement.

Ships: *Discovery, Hopewell, Halve Maen.*
Then the bridge, beautiful as any bridge, straddling the hollow
between the eyes and the gut—which loves such shapes.

2.

In sepia, the half-constructed bridge, two parts reaching.
We know the pieces fit. And the ship—we check where in the
    world she is.
A yellow isosceles gives the last known position. Between reports
and sightings we suspend a structure trusted to span the breach
—the thought is latticed, girded by gaps.

The Half Moon, a pub in
this same town, or close enough, an adjoining village.

We can't tell between the truly connected and contiguous.
We see the half and believe... *in time*—the fullness of it.

We see the moon and it gives us the sun, a memory of
    beergardenness.
The Russians probably have a name for this.

New Battersea Bridge Nocturnes

> *By using the word 'nocturne' I wished to indicate an artistic*
> *interest alone, divesting the picture of any outside anecdotal*
> *interest which might have been otherwise attached to it.*
> —James McNeill Whistler

Blue and Gold

Bogged banks, banked boats. Water like tarmac.
The bridge one long glad oblong. Slow going. Each bus
a bulb bobbing unevenly on October's early dark.
A gull. Dogs. Bold globules ahead blend to a glow.
A blonde passes by again. The air is gummy,
heavy with breath. Sight is a dulled blade now.

Blue and Silver

Not the veil of night, evening reveals villainy. Things
express their evil-twinnedness. Lines deviate, swerve,
sharpen, serrate. Living views. Vast ornate sleeves
riven of water, woven with fine metal fibres. Water thrills
at the embankment—calm, not calming.
Viciously, day is relieved of its definite edge.

Black and Gold

Blocking the bend, the bridge presents a barrier,
a hazard. Wrought band, solid and silent. A few
gilt spandrels snag the light. Dark demands

gangs of pyrotechnics—noise helps to dock thought.
An abandoned can will somehow gladden. The moon
is a sallow gong, mirrored in the glistening blanks.

Wet Season

Pictures of nothing, all alike.
—William Hazlitt on J.M.W. Turner

The world is like nothing we have ever seen,
the catastrophe of the morning's rain
hangs in the air and will not be drawn out. Yet, light.

On the horizon that has forgotten itself
and the water that refuses to own its depth
there is light.

A lone crawler toward light—
his back like a beacon on the road—that frog
that refused to budge, like light through eyelids
he sat in your mind, crawled into the space
behind your smile and sketched himself beyond your eyes.
We speak pictures of nothing in silence, quite unalike.

And the rain falls on.   Scrape, blot, wipe wet paint,
draw over. Nothing can be undone, draw over, paint on
until the canvas turns in on itself and is pierced
                              by a hole, a flame, a lake.

Lecture

To demonstrate, two large borrowed globes
from Malby's London:
                1 × continents
                1 × stars
the size of cartwheels, or a large ship's helm.

Man—moon. Tree to opposite bank.
Distance is no different
between one seaport and the next
and one planet and its neighbour—
or the sun it sails by.
It is only a matter of scales.
Space may be had by the yard.

And we can value it too, in *avoirdupois*
—each moving bulk in the night's sky—
for these are goods of weight.

The Astronomer Royal brings
the heavens to Earth,
specifically: to Suffolk.
His fingers span continents,
circle stars. A weave he would
have the worth of from the feel.

The locals clap, but cannot touch.
The globes are expensive,
have not been paid for yet.

Objection!

harshly linear
—Craig Harris reviewing *Phoenix Wright: Ace Attorney*

Before the courtroom
you go to the street

and if you are to go to the street
you must go through the door

that leads to the room
with the door to the street.

It's annoying, but let's not pretend
action isn't made of infinitely smaller actions.

You're here and then you're there,
it's just in life you forget it's all one small step.

And then the next. Slow it down enough
and you'll never cross the room.

Halfway to halfway there
you realise there was a start,

that the things you always say,
the three faces that you wear

are something that became
between beginning and being here.

How easy it is to convince ourselves
that time passes and passes us

when it's us who pass, are passing it:
this bit, this bit, then this.

A Stretch of River

Mavisbank House. Late
afternoon, winter.
The building—
what is left—rises
at the end of the long,
boggy field. It's still
quite something.

Mavis, meaning thrush.
Blackbirds and loud great tits
sing. Things, after all,
are in the habit of changing.

> There was once a camp
> for Napoleonic
> prisoners of war and so
> I've been walking along
> imagining writing to one:
> *Mon cher, ça va? But let's*
> *not talk about the war—*
> *You have tasted,*
> *you must have,*
> *this water—so sweet,*
> *so smooth, tempered*
> *by long journey from the hills,*
> *moss-filtered. It seems*
> *to remember its time*
> *as snow. The man*
> *in the wine shop*
> *told me how perfect it was*
> *for paper-making, being so soft.*
> *Yes, for many years*

they prospered
on paper, in Loanhead
and in Penicuik.

What tense to use
when writing of the future past?

Industrious Esk:
maker of men! How many
fortunes flowed from you.
There were those
who looked on Nature's might
as though it were the work
of a great and ancient general—
sought to learn from,
use, to harness it.
And many wheels
were set in motion,
and many years they moved.

Now dogs are walked here
where work was done.

'This
is the loveliest of the river's
spots.' Maidenhall Castle,
no castle left.
Where the river most
awkwardly meanders
in to virtual islets
that just demand
to be picnicked,
or settled, or paddled in.
I love the woods,
but love them most

when some manmade
but abandoned thing
is near... I find it best
not to press this sense.
A little downstream
is a lovely spot
(I recommend a trip
if you can get out)
where the cliffs shade
the sloping shore
of the opposite bank.
I sat below a tree
whose whole trunk
stretched out across the water
as though it were a limb
slung, or reaching out
to touch... something.
Leant against the base
I watched a bird,
a little treecreeper,
peck and pick
the moss away
from the bark. And with
my right eye I could also
see—beyond the far bank's
straight and upright trees—
a buzzard, high up,
describing generous circles,
slowly. And I was straining
to keep both in sight;
the distant, seeming casual
flight, the close and urgent
fretting. It was a thing
I had to try to do,
like an exercise.

Keep both in sight,
preferring neither.
Keep both in sight
and not compare
myself to either.

There was a disaster
at the gunpowder mill,
one furnace blast
triggering the next:
of course, many killed.

DANGEROUS MASONRY.
KEEP OFF. KEEP OUT.
Mavisbank House, built 1723
by William Adam and
the second Baronet
James Clerk of Penicuik.
A squarish construction,
with arms—two pavilions
moving to embrace.
Scottish style roof, but
otherwise impeccable
neo-Palladian taste.
An ornate pediment
with oriel window,
two lesser but matching sisters
on each of the side buildings.

This is on the path to Lasswade,
your side of the river. And there's
no need to tell you
that it's now no more
than a shell. But I love
the bricked up windows,

the steel bars
twice my height.

      All within a day's
      reach, even at casual pace.
      Every day I walk.
      I like the way it offers
      no new thoughts,
      only the same ones
      I had yesterday
      and those too
      seem very old.

    What I'd like to know
    is why they put you here.
    So far to drag prisoners,
    you might have escaped.
    And what do you make
    of this wild place, all castles
    and cold? Do you even know
    where you are?

Each day the same paths
or parts of paths.
The same couple
of bridges to cross
from bank to bank.
The first time
the way is a stretch
of occurrences: mill,
playground, house.
But on the way back,
things contract
to a succession of
easily accepted facts.

For days I have been
circling Mavisbank,
looping it on the map,
or taking paths that nearly
go there, routes from which
it would be only a minor
diversion. *There was a king*
who died and his men
forced a river from
its course, made up a shrine
for the deceased in the void,
heaped it with jewels,
gold, pearls—then sent
the waters rushing back.
Then they killed every slave
who'd done the work.
This was in Gibbon, I think,
but I found it elsewhere.

On discovering the house
was, latterly, used
as an asylum,
we learn nothing.
Everything that's been
learnt here will need
repacking before
we can leave, the river
folded over on itself.

I turn my back
on Mavisbank,
not having seen
one single thrush.
We must accept
stanchions, keep outs
and calls for restoration.

Tomorrow, we will not
go back to Mavisbank
to take our leave.
My dear, my time here
is ending. It was silly
to have ever written
... but I fear
all our moments
are recurring in some place.
After all, look at the signs.

Difference

All winter the river was one creature.
It shrank and expanded, but maintained
its borders. I saw to the bottom. Firm sinew.

Clear curve. I swam in it long as I could bear.
Now it is many things: muddy-shored, grass
fuzzing edges, trees that overreach

and vibrate with reflection. Insects came,
pocked the surface with legs and wings.
Then clumps of grass, detached weeds,

fur of blossoms pollen the bottom
too became confused lifting off in slicks
of mud brown trout and me

temperate following a mirrored
vapour trail an inverted bankline
green and yellow bands bobbing

beyond reach we are bodies I think and unthink

Building

After all, I could find no way to speak of myself
that was not crudely structural. Crazed, as is paving.
That is: fitting the overall format but constructed
from irregular parts. I dug deep. I found there was
no way to speak of myself that was not somehow
structural. And so I built castles in the sky,
or rather in the Alps—they being near enough.
Or rather I drew them, dreamed them. They are made
of glass, most stony of sky cladding. They are not made
of glass, most ethereal of rock. I have enclosed
a lake in lips, lapped it with crystal tongues. I have not.
I can find no way to speak of 'the self' that is not,
essentially, structural. I am building a roof above
the highest peak to keep the rain off—because it dulls my
geodesic heart. Four chambers, the flow and interplay
between parts that can find no way to speak of itself
not grossly structural. This wall, its bricks are made of air.
It's only arrangement. Or rather I imagine myself the man
who dreamt of high windows. It's a sort of sanatorium
with simple, pinewood rooms. It's a sort of shack or chalet
to think it. Damnedly structural. The mountains beyond
the balcony are, I know, and have no need to look at them.
They have no way to think of themselves, not permanently
structural. Here the air's better, or less of it. We see
more clearly. The eyes the smudgy windows of our souls.
I could find. I've schlepped the pretty parts of cathedrals,
of malls. Of lamps and underground stations. Purely
structural. No way. Each foot falls plumb to the ground.

The Egyptologist

I have succumbed to a curse that forces me to disappear.
—Hugh Evelyn White

I know of the joy that is in living; the sweet zeer of plainest water,
the sky like a woman on all fours, starred from navel to nipples.
I know the relief of the dawn, a cool cotton sheet pulled up and over,

the kindness of a breeze. I know how lucky we are to see
ourselves in everything, but bigger, stronger and forever—
though still subject to our moods. I stash treasure about me:

shade; old worlds; an alabaster, oviform box that I recall though
I cannot touch. Inside I will discover, finally, the secret
to feeling well. I know that though nothing is really numberless

I shall never exhaust all the riches to be found. I too would choose
to take the best parts with me. But I know it does not matter
how many walls, how few doors. I know I am coming for me.

I know the dead abandon all their wonderful things to the living.

Cockle Shell Beach, Low Tide

The heart breaks beneath the feet—
It is smashed into more exquisite
shapes—Crystal and... silk—
On this midden, half a tennis
ball has ceased to roll—Just rubber
now—Unsmooth as skin—Barnacles
empty beaks—A lozenge pattern
that never repeats—Thin mud
has dried to its own design—
Like the sun-hard boulder clay—
We think we know but it doesn't
tessellate—Splits uniquely—
And seen from far away—An unbroken
beige channel through blue-green fields—
Studded with pillboxes—Land borrowed
from the sea—It lets them be a while—
Rearranges the coastline instead—
Shifting the shingle into slow waves—
Singing as we go—

Labour

And once I had cleared my desk
of five years I was grimy and hot,
but it was not enough. So I undid
that rat king of scart leads,
following decades of loose ends—
I made of them little grey stooks,
fastened tight round the middle
with string, and stacked them up.
I did good work. That is what I thought
and still felt as the train passed
from city into parcelled countryside.
I think I said it had been hot. But
my sweat was dried, my nails dirty.
Through the window came the outside
all zesty with grasses freshly destroyed.

Daphnia; or, The Water Flea

Damp Tractor-rut; or, The Dried Pool. Clear Mackintosh;
or, A Chitting Seed. Single-eyed; or, Simple-heartedly. An
Unfixable Scent; or, Umbrella Jerking. Coy Head; or, The
Beaked Nub. Bracketed Thought; or, The Puddled Scene.

In the river I know nothing of the water flea. That is a tale
best told in a doorway, on a wet afternoon, waiting.

Mossed Roof-tile; or, Familiar Aliens. Tight Liquid; or, Deep
Sedimentary. Persistent Creature; or, The Water Flea. A Long
Pause; or, The End.

In Praise of Pollen

So, someone claps their hands and all the feetless things of
    the world
spring to attention. An infectious delight; the air thick with
    spores, enough
wayward hope to exceed chance. This is the healthy
    flourishing that grizzles
at the nose and throat. All that had hugged to itself in the
    cold recalls it's a sin
not to meet the sun with the appropriate degree of
    enthusiasm. Everything
spills over like a litterbin. Smells spread further. A sticky
    abundance. Even
our ears buzz with joy. Bring the bees, wasps, flies. Be happy.
    Drag the days
out on to the streets, shuck the rain from the plastic chairs.
    The tarmac hums
and the measly strip of common is now more than I can take.
    My lungs
express this—when they can get a word in—the choking
    flurry of excess sex,
a thoughtless jubilation around and in and of me, even as I
    shake my head.

Four Seasons, St Giles Cripplegate

Time is upon us and so few days are ours entirely
in the slip of our mid-to-late-twenties. A hard sun
drives us to this hushed cool. St Giles is a very old
church. Here a string ensemble sometimes rehearse
and today rehearse. Strong breezes stirred these stones.
Three times they have built, rebuilt, partially rebuilt.
The church is quite old. The lead violin calls the players
to halt, to start from the middle: 'Again, more drunk this time.'
We will listen and leave before the end, go and drink,
as so often, practising our giddy autumnal theme. That music
is quite old. When all our work is done, our harvests in
—we are quite old/quite young—we will be ready then.

Notes and Acknowledgments

'Notes: A Monumental Brass' takes ideas and phrases from the 'Two Women and their Monumental Brass, c. 1480', an essay by Judith M. Bennett published in the *Journal of the British Archaeological Association*; all the insights and accuracies are hers, all the follies my own.

'Wet Season' came second in the 2009 International Edwin Morgan Poetry Competition and was included in my pamphlet *Natural Histories* (Salt, 2011). It has been pointed out the epigraph by Hazlitt should actually read '… and very like'. I believe I discovered it in a book by Gilles Deleuze and it is warped by the translation out of and back into English—or I misread it. Either way, I choose to retain this happy accident. The last lines are also a corruption of words from a Deleuze essay in translation.

I am immensely grateful for the generosity of the Hawthornden Foundation, for a Fellowship in 2012, and to The Society of Authors, for an Eric Gregory Award in 2014.

Thanks are due to the editors and publishers of the following magazines and anthologies where some of these poems, or versions of them, have previously appeared: *Ambit*; *Coin Opera II: Fulminare's Revenge*, ed. Kirsten Irving and Jon Stone (Sidekick Books, 2013); *Days of Roses* website; *Dear World and Everyone In It: New Poetry in the UK*, ed. Nathan Hamilton (Bloodaxe, 2013); *Glass Cases and Curios: Poetry & Art Inspired by Museums*, ed. Karen Harvey and Leanne Moden (2013); the *Guardian*'s 'Poem of the Week'; *Magma*; *London Review of Books*; *Other Countries: Contemporary Poets Rewiring History*, ed. Claire Trévien and Gareth Prior (2014); *Oxford Poetry*; *Penning Perfumes: An Anthology of Scent Inspired Poetry*, ed. Claire Trévien (Fast Culture/Scratch and Sniff, 2012); *Poems in Which*; *Poetry London*; *The Rialto*; *The Salt Book of Younger Poets*, ed. Roddy Lumsden and Eloise Stonborough (Salt, 2011); *Transom*; *Warwick Review*; *Wild Court*.

My huge thanks to the embarrassingly large number of people who have supported me with invaluable advice and encouragement over many years. Particular thanks must go to the following: Polly Atkin, Paul Batchelor, James Brookes, John Canfield, John Clegg, Kayo Chingonyi, Joey Connolly, Andrew Forster, Mischa Foster Poole, Isabel Galleymore, Dai George, Holly Hopkins, Michael Hulse, Amy Key, Frances Leviston, Éireann Lorsung, Roddy Lumsden and his Wednesday Group, Kathryn Maris, David Morley, Rebecca Perry, Rachel Piercey, Eileen Pun, Declan Ryan, Martha Sprackland, Eloise Stonborough, Claire Trévien, Aime Williams and Chrissy Williams.

I would like to thank all the staff at Pavilion, especially Deryn Rees-Jones for her belief in my work and careful editing.

Love and thanks to my family for never once questioning the bizarre impulse that led me to pursue poetry. And thanks to Jenny Holden and Chris Larkin, who teach me to love the world.